PERSONAL GROWTH AND SUCCESS JOURNAL

PERSONAL GROWTH AND SUCCESS JOURNAL

Exercises and Affirmations
to Motivate Your Next
Big Achievements

CANDY MOTZEK, CPCC, PCC

ROCKRIDGE
PRESS

For general information on our other products and services or to obtain technical support, please contact our Customer Care Department within the United States at (866) 744-2665, or outside the United States at (510) 253-0500.

Rockridge Press publishes its books in a variety of electronic and print formats. Some content that appears in print may not be available in electronic books, and vice versa.

Interior and Cover Designer: Tess Evans
Art Producer: Janice Ackerman
Editor: Chloe Moffett
Production Editor: Dylan Julian
Production Manager: David Zapanta

Illustration: Courtesy of Creative Market. Author Photo Courtesy of Ian Redd, Vancouver Headshots.

Paperback ISBN: 978-1-63878-122-6
R0

THIS JOURNAL BELONGS TO:

CONTENTS

INTRODUCTION

HI THERE! Welcome to my little corner of the world. I've structured this journal to be like my life-coaching sessions. These sessions are casual conversations filled with deep, thought-provoking questions. I lovingly guide my clients to understand what they most want out of life and how to get it.

Each of us has personal definitions of fulfillment and success. Your way of thinking about success is different from mine, and the way you think of success 10 years from now will be different from your ideas about it today. And that's exactly as it should be.

I've been a coach for close to a decade and many of these journal prompts and exercises are the same ones I share with my amazing clients. Hundreds of my clients have gone from feeling lost, overwhelmed, and burned-out to feeling fulfilled and excited about their life and the possibilities in front of them. You can, too.

To get started, intentionally create your personal sanctuary. Start with the basics: a chair and writing table form the backbone of your sacred space. I like to surround myself with plants, crystals, and a fuzzy blanket (in case I get cold). You might also consider keeping a candle close by to light during morning journaling sessions, like I do. Find objects and a routine that feel good to you. The act of creating your own oasis will help you deepen your journaling practice while lending you a feeling of safety and relaxation.

I recommend then setting aside 10 to 15 minutes to reflect every day. These small daily reflection sessions will yield far more satisfaction and success than an all-or-nothing rush. Grab this journal and a couple of your favorite pens and turn the page.

Start at the beginning and work through the journal sequentially. At first, your journal will look fresh and new. With time, the cover will get bent and stained and the pages will wrinkle and wear. The more worn the journal is, the deeper your clarity will be and the more empowered you will feel.

My heartfelt wish is for you to experience a life filled with love, health, and success, however you choose to define it. Let's get started.

THE MEANING OF SUCCESS

WHAT IS SUCCESS? I believe it's both the journey and the destination. Life is like climbing a mountain. The big dream is to reach the summit, but the time spent on the trail offers satisfaction and joy, too.

On every hike, there are places where you pause to take in the view. Sometimes you look out to the sunset across the valley or pass a cool mountain stream. When walking through the woods, you experience the fresh air and deep green silence.

There might be times during a hike when you suspect you took a wrong turn, or you feel lost. No one wants to make a mistake or fail. How does failure, or the times you're exhausted and overwhelmed, fit into your journey? They are all part of the same hiking trip.

When hiking, you are likely to get sweaty and grimy. Your pack might feel heavier today than it did yesterday; your back gets sore sometimes, too. You might even drop something along the path. This is all part of the experience. Keep going and decide how you will think about and frame any setbacks. You can complain, compare yourself to others, decide it's unfair, and feel upset. Or you can decide this, too, is part of your journey.

You still see those same viewpoints with or without failure along the way. Your interpretation will frame your perspective. Can you choose to see growth, progress, and learning throughout? Success isn't just a perfect relationship, a degree from your school of choice, or a good job with a large salary. Success is who you are and how you feel about yourself. The only thing 100 percent in your control is how you process and interpret the circumstances of your life.

So where are you on your success journey? The good news is that, wherever you are right now, and no matter what you're going through, you're already well on your way. You may have picked this journal up to help you through a hard time, or maybe you're just feeling stuck. I'm here to remind you that you've already started the journey up the mountain; this journal is just your next step to success.

A BIRD'S-EYE VIEW OF YOUR LIFE

> *"Just be yourself. Let people see the real, imperfect, flawed, quirky, weird, beautiful, and magical person that you are."*
>
> —MANDY HALE

YOU ARE HERE. WHERE IS HERE?

Let's get an overview of the level of your success and satisfaction in your life today. Now, this is NOT a serious exercise, so, before you begin, stand up and shake off the tension. Yes, literally shake your hands, wiggle your shoulders, and get your blood moving. Feeling energized? Okay, let's dive in.

Note: There is no wrong answer; there is only *your* answer.

1. Grab some colored pencils, markers, or highlighters.

2. Ask this question for each key area: "On a scale of 1 to 10, how satisfied am I in this area?" (1 = Terribly unsatisfied, 10 = Blissfully satisfied).

3. Write the first number that pops into your mind in the square.

4. Fill in the number of squares to show your current score.

5. Finally, draw a continuous line connecting the score of each area.

AREA	#/10										
CAREER/SCHOOL/ BUSINESS	6										
HEALTH	5										
MONEY	8										
FUN AND RECREATION	7										
FRIENDS	3										
FAMILY	9										
LOVE/SIGNIFI- CANT OTHER	2										
PERSONAL DEVELOPMENT	4										

Now it's your turn:

AREA	#/10										
CAREER/SCHOOL/ BUSINESS											
HEALTH											
MONEY											
FUN AND RECREATION											
FRIENDS											
FAMILY											
LOVE/SIGNIFI- CANT OTHER											
PERSONAL DEVELOPMENT											

Good work! This is a bird's-eye view of your current level of satisfaction. Your ratings will change with time, but trust that they are accurate for you today.

What do you notice about your line and the distribution of numbers? Are the numbers all high or low? Do they vary widely? Is your line smooth and even or bumpy and jagged? What one word would you use to describe your diagram?

Mentally step back, release any judgments, and get curious. Are there any areas in which your rating was a surprise? Do you notice a trend? Do you think that if the rating in one area increased dramatically, it would be reflected in other areas?

It's normal to second-guess yourself. It is natural to want to avoid making mistakes or looking anything other than perfect. What was it like to listen to yourself and trust your intuition to accurately rate your satisfaction today?

As you look at the diagram, is there one area that you keep thinking of? Why do you think that is? Could focusing on this area have a ripple effect on the other areas? What one thing could you do today to improve that area?

EVERY DAY CAN BE EXTRAORDINARY

IT'S TIME FOR YOU TO BELIEVE IN YOURSELF AGAIN.

Can an average day still be incredible? Is it possible to experience something magical every day of your life? You get to choose. List three reasons why or why not.

1.

2.

3.

Is today a day like any other? Even though it might feel like a repeat, or like any old "nothing special" day, when you get curious, you can find something that lifts your spirits. What is that one thing for you today?

It feels good to remember excellent days and personal stories. What's one of your favorites? A summer day, a campfire under the stars, or maybe a special holiday? What one specific memory do you treasure about your last excellent day?

Scent is a powerful emotional trigger. One whiff is the fastest path directly to your brain. Do you have a favorite aroma from childhood? Maybe it's vanilla from baking or the scent of peonies in the warm spring sun. What scent conjures up a fond memory?

How much fun can one day hold? It's completely up to you. Decide that you will create an excellent day sometime within the next week. Grab your calendar, choose a day, and start planning it below. What will you do? Describe the fun you will have.

How is the plan for your fun day going? Build the anticipation and enjoy the planning as much as you enjoy the day itself. Create a custom playlist for your fun day. Name the playlist, add your favorite songs, and begin enjoying the tunes now.

A PERFECTLY AVERAGE DAY

How do you bridge the gap between your current life and a life you can only dream of? It starts with a vision. Success in your life is based on the quality of all of your combined days.

What would an average day look like in your ideal life? Write a detailed letter describing your future self and this average day. Use the space below to get started, or write in a separate journal or on some nice stationery.

- What time do you get up?

- What do you do?

- Where do you go?

- Who are you with?

- What is your evening like?

- How does your home look?

- What is the vibe?

- What emotions do you sense?

- What sounds and smells fill the air?

- How do you talk to yourself as you go about your day running errands, working, and interacting with your friends and loved ones?

90-DAY GROWTH GOAL

> *"Life takes on meaning when you become motivated, set goals, and charge after them."*
>
> —LES BROWN

The search for success is often sparked when life feels flat, boring, or like a never-ending grind. When was the last time you tried something new or set a fresh goal to grow?

Go-to goals are often restrictive and chosen because there is a belief that there's a problem to be fixed (for example, lose twenty pounds, or stop smoking). Focus on a goal that encourages growth over the next 90 days. Your growth goal could be to learn a new language, master a new hobby, run or walk every day, or start a yoga practice. Brainstorm ideas here.

Review the list you brainstormed. Eliminate all potential goals that have the word "should" or a feeling of obligation. This growth goal is not meant to "fix you." Which of your ideas make you excited and energized? Why? Use the space below to record your thoughts, and then narrow down your list to three top contenders.

1.

2.

3.

Run each of your top three growth-goal contenders through these filtering questions, and then choose the goal you're most excited about.

- *Does it sound interesting and feel like "you"?*

- *How long have you been wanting to do this?*

- *How do you think you will feel when you achieve it?*

My 90-day growth goal is:

A SMART goal is Specific, Measurable, Achievable, Relevant, and Time-bound.

NON-SMART GOAL: *"I will start running."*

SMART VERSION: *"I will run on my treadmill for 30 minutes, three times every week for the next three months."*

Brainstorm how to make your 90-day growth goal SMART.

What small, consistent steps can you start making this week? Start by making a list. For example: *"What do I need to do to easily run a 5k by June 30th? Buy running shoes, find a training plan, etc."*

VISUALIZE YOUR 90-DAY GROWTH GOAL

Visualizing is a handy tool to solve problems, obtain resources, and reach your 90-day growth goal more easily.

Close your eyes and imagine your kitchen. Think of walking to the fridge and opening the door. What's on the top shelf right now? Imagine taking something out and placing it on the counter. Now close the door.

Do you see how easy that was? Now, create a movie scene in your mind's eye of you reaching your growth goal. Watch the minute details play across the screen of your imagination. See yourself sharing with someone the news that you completed your goal. Who are you telling? How are you dressed? What time of day is it? Cultivate and lock in the emotions of achievement, pride, victory, and enjoyment. Play that movie in your mind morning and night.

COMPELLING REASON

"Giving up on your goal because of one setback is like slashing your other three tires because you got a flat."

—MEL ROBBINS

Keep your 90-Day Growth Goal at the front of your mind. Connect with it daily. This is one of the best ways to remember what you're striving for. What progress have you made so far?

Take a moment to reflect on your past. In what areas have you been successful in achieving goals? When did you quit on yourself or just plain forget? How would your life change for the better if you learned how to set goals and achieve them?

On a scale of 1 to 10, how much do you believe you will reach this 90-day growth goal? It's completely normal to harbor some self-doubt. Use this space to reassure yourself. You may not have done this before, but I believe you can figure it out.

Why is this goal the best one for you to work on right now? Find at least three reasons and, as you respond, consider how you will grow, what you will learn, and what these new skills will allow you to do in the future.

Who do you know that could use support in reaching their goals, too? How can you partner with them to stay committed and follow through? For example, you could agree to send each other a text every day that includes progress updates and cheerful encouragement.

Reward progress. Break your growth goal into chunks and reward yourself every step of the way. Make a list of the checkpoints below. How will you reward yourself? You could play a video game, give yourself a night off, or buy a new houseplant.

TELL ME WHY

Create a compelling reason to keep striving for your growth goal no matter what happens. Sometimes, you'll be making great progress and then run into a roadblock. When life happens, don't give up in frustration and impatience.

Why do you want this goal? What is the reason, the driver, the thing that you will use to motivate yourself to keep going? Once you've answered, ask "why?" again. Keep going. Don't stop writing. Ask "why?" several times. This deep dive will connect you to your compelling reason.

WHY?	
WHY DO I WANT THIS?	
WHY IS THIS IMPORTANT?	
WHY DOES IT MATTER?	
MY COMPELLING REASON:	

SUCCESS ROLE MODEL

"I want to inspire people. I want someone to look at me and say, 'Because of you I didn't give up.'"

—UNKNOWN

How do you measure success? More money, more health, more love, more fun and adventure? What are three specific ways you will decide to measure your success?

1.

2.

3.

At its core, success is an emotion. Goals and dreams are viewed as important because it is believed that they will make you *feel* successful. How else will you feel when you reach your dream? How have past accomplishments made you feel? (Confident? Empowered? Fulfilled? Inspired?)

Who is a role model you look up to? It may be someone famous or someone you know in real life. Why do you admire them? What is it about them and what they've achieved that is meaningful and inspiring to you? Name and describe this person below.

Take time to turn the tables and acknowledge yourself. When have you been someone else's role model? Where has someone else looked up to you as an example of what is possible? What characteristics do you already have that make you a good example to others?

Your natural strengths may come easily to you, but that doesn't mean they are easy for everyone else. Be bold, capture your strengths on paper, and you will start to realize how amazing you already are. List some of your strengths and explain how they've helped you.

The phrase "I AM" is powerful. Now that you've identified some of your strengths, blend them into "I AM" statements and write them below.

Example:

STRENGTHS: kind and caring

STATEMENT: I AM a kind and caring friend.

DEAR FUTURE ME

Once you've chosen your growth goal, use this fun ritual to set it in motion and manifest it into reality. Start by buying a beautiful note card. Early in the morning, before sunrise, or late at night, light a candle and play some inspiring music. Use the box-breathing technique (see page 38) to become present and get centered.

Write a heartfelt note to your future self. Describe your growth goal *as if it is already done*. Describe how you feel and what life is like. End the note with *"I give my word that I will create this or something better."* Address the envelope and mail it to yourself. On the envelope make a note: *"Do not open until _____,"* a date 90 days in the future.

Open the envelope on the 90-day anniversary and read what you wrote. Reflect on your growth and what you've accomplished. Consider how you have welcomed more success, love, connection, and abundance into your life.

THESE THREE THINGS

"You will never change your life until you change something you do daily. The secret of your success is found in your daily routine."

—JOHN C. MAXWELL

It is common to believe that you must do everything correctly to be successful. Do you believe you need to perform perfectly (and right away) to reach the next step of success? Why?

Being in a rush can limit your resourcefulness. Gently and kindly ask yourself if you're so busy that you forgot where you're heading. Where would you like to go? What needs to change for you to get there?

Box breathing works well to diffuse your nervous energy. Inhale to the count of four, hold your breath for a count of four, exhale slowly to the count of four, and hold empty for the count of four. Repeat this four-by-four breathing cycle three times for the best results. Write about how you felt before you tried this technique and how you felt afterward.

What is the one most important step you can take today toward your growth goal? What did you uncover by asking this one powerful question? Did your answer seem too simple? Did you have trouble choosing just one thing? Asking and answering this question every day will sharpen your response and your results.

List five potential challenges or barriers to completing your daily steps toward your goal. Then strategize one way to overcome each of them.

What are you learning about yourself and your drive for success? Stick with the "one question" approach for three more days. How are your answers changing, if at all?

THESE THREE THINGS

Manage your time, energy, and productivity with this simple and powerful approach. Every morning, ask, *"What are the three most important things I can do today to move toward my goal?"* Then do them. That's it.

It seems simple, but small, consistent steps create greatness. Three actions today hardly seem worthwhile. But look at how the numbers grow. After a month, it's almost 100. At the end of a year, you will have taken more than 1,000 deliberate and highly effective steps toward your goals. Build this habit to make fast progress and to build self-trust.

Make a promise to yourself and keep it. Starting today, choose and write down three things each day, then do them, check them off your list, and appreciate that you did what you set out to do. Soon you will be amazed at your progress and others will begin asking you, *"What's your secret?"*

SELF-CARE

I WILL TAKE THE INITIATIVE TO GIVE MYSELF WHAT I NEED TO THRIVE.

Self-care is not just bubble baths and pedicures. How would you define self-care? Do you include it in your day? Have you forgotten to make yourself a priority?

It can be hard admitting that you're exhausted, but sometimes that acknowledgment is the exact step needed to begin working toward a refreshing life. Write honestly about how you've been feeling lately. Are you ready to make a change?

Admitting you are exhausted is the first step to integrating self-care into your day. Prioritizing resilience will prime your pump for success. It is common to delay taking care of your own needs. Describe how this delay may have helped or hindered you in the past. What are you learning now?

If you're not yet ready to put yourself at the top of the list, what's holding you back? Write down five possible answers to that question. Are you too busy at work or with your kids? Is money too tight? Maybe you just don't know *how* to prioritize yourself.

A self-care practice is highly individual. Doing an activity you enjoy for just five minutes can make a difference. Brainstorm some quick self-care practices. For example, you could put on a favorite song and dance it out or spend a few minutes crafting.

Which self-care practices did you try? How did you feel afterward? Write about any changes you noticed. Was it worth the time? What will you do next?

CREATE YOUR SELF-CARE PRESCRIPTION

If you were a cell phone, you would want to keep your batteries fully charged. In some ways you are like your cell phone, and one approach to recharging your batteries is through self-care. Self-care and success go hand in hand. Use this space to list 10 or so potential self-care activities.

Ready for a challenge? Using the list you wrote, try one activity a day for the next month, repeating the ones you most enjoyed. Keep track below and add a star to the activities you enjoyed. At the end of 30 days, you will have created your customized self-care plan.

	ACTIVITY	STAR THE ONES YOU ENJOYED	(DONE)
1			
2			
3			
4			
5			
6			
7			
8			
9			
10			

BODY, MIND, SPIRIT

MY BODY IS HEALTHY, MY MIND CALM, MY SOUL SATISFIED.

Do you intentionally balance the aspects of your body, mind, and spirit? Are you generally in balance or not? How does this balance, or lack thereof, affect you?

Nourish your body with healthy food, water, fresh air, and natural surroundings. What foods make your body feel well nourished? What do you notice when you've stayed hydrated? What surroundings promote a feeling of well-being, and how do they help you live your best life?

What is your healthiest habit in caring for your body? Describe how you feel when you practice it. When was the last time you added a new healthy habit? What was it and why did you choose it?

Sleep is an often-ignored component of health and creativity. How many hours a night do you sleep? What's the quality of your sleep? Do you fall asleep quickly? If not, why not? What is one thing you can do to improve this area of your life?

Your thoughts are powerful, and they can help or hurt you. One of the ways to enhance your mindset is to limit your consumption of social media and sensational news. Consider taking a "social media vacation" for one day this week and reflect on your experience.

Spirit is highly individual, and it is what you make it. What do you think it is? What does balance in spirit mean to you? Is it practicing your faith just a little bit more, acting through service and kindness, or spending more time in nature?

SHIFTING INTO BALANCE

The story you tell yourself about creating mind-body-spirit balance matters. Notice that balance does not mean "precisely the same." Balance is dynamic. At times, keeping a healthy balance is easy and natural; at other times it's a struggle. Try this exercise to demonstrate to yourself how a slight physical shift can make a significant difference to your balance.

POSITION	ON A SCALE OF 1 TO 10, HOW EASY IS IT TO STAY BALANCED? (1 = NOT EASY, 10 = VERY EASY)
STAND COMFORTABLY UPRIGHT	
REMAIN STANDING AND CLOSE YOUR EYES.	
NOW, OPEN YOUR EYES AND LIFT ONE FOOT OFF THE GROUND.	
KEEPING YOUR FOOT OFF THE GROUND, CLOSE YOUR EYES AGAIN.	

Pay attention to how the dynamic of balance shifts with the slightest physical adjustment. Note any other sensations you experience.

These small shifts can help you maintain a mind-body-spirit balance, too. Awareness is everything. Begin by noticing where you are moving off balance. You may notice it as a mood swing, feeling tired, or an increase in stress.

Use this powerful question when you find yourself off-balance: *"What small adjustment can I make today to restore my equilibrium?"*

DAY

I AM FAR MORE CAPABLE THAN I KNOW; I WILL FIGURE THIS OUT.

Gratitude is a powerful force for good. Say "thank you" out loud each day before you get out of bed. How do you feel?

Not a morning person? Think you don't have time to journal in the morning? Think again. Respond to this question and change your day. What do you want to make time for today? What is the priority and why?

Starting your day from an intentional space will put you squarely in control of how you experience your everyday circumstances. What will you do to set yourself up for success today? Why is this important, and what impact will it have?

Set your timer for five minutes, sip your morning tea or coffee, and answer this prompt. What are you looking forward to today? When you feel good, you will attract even more goodness into your life.

Is today going to be difficult? Outline all the things that will be challenging today. Then, at the end, write this affirmation: *"I am far more capable than I know; I will figure this out."*

Sometimes you can benefit from starting the day with a dose of self-love and nurture. Grab your pen and answer the question, *"What does my spirit need more of today, and how will I make this happen?"*

THIS IS NOT A TO-DO LIST

Overwhelmed with too many things to do and the day hasn't even begun? Writing in a journal helps make space so you can think more clearly.

First, this is NOT a to-do list. Write down everything you need to accomplish today. List every task, big and small. When you think you're done, keep your pen moving, doodling for a minute or two, and you will likely discover items to add to your list. Add those items, as well.

When the list is done, *just look at it.* These items are what have been weighing on your mind. Writing them down is like cleaning out your junk drawer. You may find that you feel clearer, cleaner, and more squarely in control of what you will do next.

NIGHT AND SLEEP

I RELEASE TODAY AND GIVE MYSELF PERMISSION TO REST AND RENEW.

Cultivate a good night's sleep with your nighttime routine. What would your days be like if you slept like a log and woke up refreshed?

Describe your current bedtime routine. You may have fallen into an unhealthy habit, and that's okay. Start by taking inventory. Write out all the details, including when you normally go to bed. Do you sleep with your phone? Are you rushing around until the last minute?

Do you have problems falling asleep? Do you toss and turn? If you lie awake in the middle of the night, what is that like? Do you hit the snooze button repeatedly before dragging yourself out of bed? Describe an average night's sleep so you can better recognize your patterns.

Blue light from digital screens disrupts sleep hormone production. Turn off the TV and put your devices away 30 to 60 minutes before you go to sleep. How do you feel about this recommendation? Describe any resistance and what happens when you try this approach.

This journal can help clear your mind and ready it for sleep. When you've had a stressful day, use this space to vent. What made the day hard? Why is it bothering you? What could you say to yourself to let it go?

This journal can help you prepare for tomorrow so your mind can relax and fall asleep. What do you need to do tomorrow? Is there something you're worried you might forget? Get it on paper.

FALL ASLEEP MINDFULLY

Use this body scan meditation to release tension, relax your entire body, and promote more restful sleep. This practice entails checking in, nonjudgmentally, with every part of your body.

1. Lie down in bed, on your back, and get comfortable.

2. Breathe. Focus on the air moving in and out of your lungs.

3. Bring your awareness to your feet and observe all the sensations there.

4. Visualize releasing any discomfort or difficult emotions that bubble up from that area. Allow the discomfort to be washed away by your breath.

5. Next, move your attention to your ankles and repeat this process.

6. Slowly move your attention up your body until you either fall asleep or reach the top of your head.

After trying this for a few nights, has it helped with your sleep? Have you noticed any other effects?

LESS STRESS, MORE SUCCESS

REST AND RELAXATION ARE A GIFT I GIVE MYSELF DAILY.

Is stress an ever-present companion? Do you think it's possible to be successful with less stress? Why or why not?

Two different ends of the *subjective* stress spectrum are eustress and distress. Eustress feels helpful, as it promotes growth. Distress feels negative. Riding a roller coaster is fun, exhilarating, and thrilling for some; others would say it's terrifying. How do you distinguish good stress from bad stress?

What is eustress now can become distress later, depending on your perspective. Cultivating the mind-body-spirit balance will build your resilience. Can you think of an example where something you may have called eustress became distress after a time? Describe your experience and why you think it changed.

The four common sources of stress are relationships, money, health concerns, and work.

Your body responds to stress with the fight, flight, or freeze response. These responses are physiological reactions meant to keep you safe. What's your most common response? To fight? Run away? Freeze?

Do you have healthy strategies for managing stress? Create a list of ones you've tried and any you'd like to try in the future. For example, you might exercise, breathe deeply, meditate, talk it out with a friend, listen to music, or watch a comedy.

Try this approach to make a stressful day more manageable. Imagine you are the most optimistic and positive person you've ever met. Step into that person's perspective and describe the day to yourself. What shifts for you when you try this alternate viewpoint?

YOUR EARLY STRESS WARNING SIGNALS

How you manage stress (distress), especially when it becomes recurring stress, is important because it can affect your physical health. Left unchecked, stress can manifest into chronic illness.

When stress builds up in your life, does your stomach hurt or your neck get tight? Being aware of how excess, and potentially harmful, stress shows up in your body will help you flag your early warning signs and remind you to apply some stress management.

Mark on the drawing where you physically experience stress. Draw an arrow to point to the figure's back if that is an area where you experience stress.

What stress reduction techniques will you try the next time you're stressed? Plan now so you'll be prepared the next time you need relief.

CLEAR THE CLUTTER

"Discard anything that doesn't spark joy."

—MARIE KONDO

Do you have a place for everything? Or is everything scattered all over the place? Look around you with fresh eyes and describe what you see.

Get curious about any clutter you've allowed into your space. What purpose does it serve? Does it help you avoid something else that is even more uncomfortable? How might clutter be helping you?

Clutter is like having too many apps open on your phone or computer. Start with one area (it could be your desk or your nightstand) and take a photo. This is your "before." Set a timer for 15 minutes and clean it up. Why did you choose this area, and how do you think decluttering will add to your progress?

Now take the "after" photo and compare the two. How do you feel having completed that task? Are you amazed at how much you accomplished, or are you overwhelmed by all that remains to be done? Does breaking up cleaning into smaller chunks help you get it done?

Eavesdrop on your thoughts and write them here. "That wasn't too bad," "I can see my table now," or "I have so far to go." Choose one supportive thought to help you continue making progress. Use this supportive thought to remind yourself that you can do this!

Clutter can cause stress, resulting in the release of the stress hormone cortisol, which can contribute to weight gain and chronic illnesses over time. How could clutter be adding to your stress levels? Does the condition of your space support your dreams?

10 X 10 LET IT GO! CLEAR IT OUT!

Having more "stuff" means having more to maintain, clean, and organize, which takes time, money, and energy that you could be using toward your growth goal. Do a 10 x 10 challenge and clear out 100 things from your space.

Here's what you need:

- Box for donations
- Garbage bag
- Recycling bin

You are going to clear 10 things from 10 different spaces. Examples include:

- Your computer
- Mobile phone
- Bathroom
- Kitchen
- Bedroom
- Living area
- Car
- Bedroom closet
- Kid's room
- Laundry room
- Storage area
- Carport or garage
- Front or backyard
- Entryway

Do it all in one afternoon, or tackle one area a day for the next 10 days. Have fun with this; put on some music and dive in.

HOW TO HANDLE DISAPPOINTMENT

I WANT TO SEE WHAT HAPPENS IF I DON'T GIVE UP.

Sometimes no matter what you do, things don't work out. How do you handle disappointment and discouragement when this happens? How does knowing your response help with your 90-day goal?

Move beyond a painful feeling by naming it, pinpointing the emotion for your brain, and saying, "This *emotion* is how I'm feeling." Now it's no longer a mystery. Write it in big, bold, capital letters and underline it, too!

When you resist an emotion, it persists. The easiest way to overcome discomfort is to be present with the feeling. Which emotion are you willing to sit with now? Write about it. Describe how it feels and what you're thinking. Now that it's on paper, do you feel differently?

When you feel better, you'll be able to think better, too. Once you've allowed the painful feeling and your fight-or-flight reaction has lessened, you'll be able to find new ways of approaching the same challenge. Have you had any new insights? Capture them here.

Life is not all or nothing. It's not either working or not working. Train your brain to find new evidence. Ask a compelling question and find the answer. For example, when you think nothing's working, try, *"How is it possible that it's actually working?"*

Create a backup plan. Who could you ask for help next time you're facing a challenge? What tools or resources could you use? Find a new thought to lean on for encouragement. Maybe you could try a new strategy. Outline your plan.

THE LIGHTER SIDE OF DISCOMFORT

What if there really is only *one* thing getting in your way? What if that thing is you trying to avoid being uncomfortable? By trying to avoid discomfort, you delay your progress toward your dreams and goals.

Discomfort is the currency for success. It's true that when you dive in and are willing to feel uncomfortable, you will experience frustration and disappointment, *but* you will also create more results so much faster. You will learn and grow and become the kind of person who reaches their goals, no matter what.

This week, play discomfort bingo. When you create a line, reward yourself with something fun!

B	I	N	G	O
You said "hi" to a stranger	You asked yourself, "How am I feeling?"	Someone acknowledged you and you said "thank you"	You tried something new	You paused instead of giving a quick retort
You expressed your opinion	You told someone you were having a tough day and asked for a hug	When you felt discomfort, you named the emotion	You comforted yourself when you were feeling blue	When feeling frustrated, you took a breath and counted to 10
When feeling stressed, you relaxed instead of pushing yourself harder	You spoke your truth	FREE SPACE	You stood still in a busy store, caught people's eyes, and smiled at them	You tidied up a cluttered space
You took a 10-minute break outside for fresh air	You smiled and said "thank you"	You paused to breathe	You told someone you appreciate them	You asked someone for help with something small
You allowed yourself to feel bored	You got an "urgent" request and resisted responding ASAP	You moved for five minutes when you felt angry	You gave a genuine apology when you missed the mark	You offered up a random act of kindness

CONNECTION

**I WILL FOCUS MY ENERGY ON
RELATIONSHIPS THAT NOURISH
AND SUPPORT ME.**

Make a list of all the people you've seen or connected with in the past week. What
were the highlights? Why did you enjoy them?

Humans are social beings. Relationships, laughter, and connection all add to feeling successful. Consider some of the intangible, everyday abundance you experience because of the people you surround yourself with. What friendships and relationships make your life richer? Why?

Have you and your friends/family fallen into a rut? Say "yes" to having more fun and creating better connections. Games are a great way to lighten the mood. Brainstorm a list of your favorite games or activities as well as some new ones you would like to try.

Do you sometimes forget to ask for what you need? This can be a source of discontent in any relationship. You may think the other person *should* know what you need, but they don't; they are not mind readers. What needs do you have that you can clearly communicate?

It is common to have relationships that you value, yet somehow time has passed, and you've lost touch. Maybe you keep meaning to reach out—to call or text—but you feel embarrassed that it's been so long. Who would you like to reconnect with? Why?

Do you have a relationship in which you need to mend some fences? Maybe you said something hurtful, or they did, and now it's just *awkward*. What could you say to make amends? Often it starts with the two words "I'm sorry." Use this space to begin the conversation.

STRENGTHEN CONNECTION THROUGH APPRECIATION .

You can improve your relationships with intentional appreciation. Write a heartfelt love note and build a deeper connection with someone you love or look up to. You don't have to share it with them, but, of course, you can if you want to. In this hand-written note, describe why you appreciate them, what qualities they have that you admire, and how they have inspired you. Why do they make the world a better place and how are you a better "you" because they are part of your life? Why are you thankful that they are part of your life? What lessons have they taught you that you have paid forward?

Dear   ,

CELEBRATION (PRIDE)

"Make the most of yourself by fanning the tiny, inner sparks of possibility into flames of achievement."

—GOLDA MEIR

Celebrating your achievements releases dopamine, the happy hormone, in your brain. How often do you celebrate achieving your personal goals? How do you celebrate?

What happens when someone gives you a compliment or tells you, *"Wow, that's amazing; you're wonderful."* Do you say *"thank you"* and allow the good feelings in? Or do you mumble "It's no big deal" and then try to avoid the spotlight at all costs?

Motivation and success are created by your mindset. Create more opportunities to feel successful by celebrating. Write about five wins from the past week (big or small), then stand up and read them out loud to yourself.

Share one success with a friend or family member. After you share, ask them what they're celebrating, too. Create your own unofficial cheering squad. What can you share today? Who will you share with?

Remember when you used to get a gold star for schoolwork? It's a fun way to remind yourself how well you're doing. Buy a pack of gold stars and stick them to the pages of this journal. How do you feel when you acknowledge yourself in this way?

Celebrating wins gives you feedback about what works and doesn't work. This input will help you more easily tweak your actions and reach your goal. What have your wins revealed? What will you improve in order to move toward your goal?

BE PROUD

What are you proud of? Being too humble doesn't serve anyone, and it stops you from playing big! I know that you've done some amazing things in your life. Of course, there will always be more to do—more challenges, more problems to solve, more goals to strive for—but you can still enjoy the things you've already accomplished.

You may be resistant, but do it anyway. This is not a time to be humble; it's an opportunity to cheer for yourself.

List 50 things that you are proud of.

1. I graduated from high school   11.

2. I got my driver's license   12.

3. I am a kind and caring friend   13.

4. I asked for a raise   14.

5.   15.

6.   16.

7.   17.

8.   18.

9.   19.

10.   20.

21.

22.

23.

24.

25.

26.

27.

28.

29.

30.

31.

32.

33.

34.

35.

36.

37.

38.

39.

40.

41.

42.

43.

44.

45.

46.

47.

48.

49.

50.

FEELING JOY

"Sometimes your joy is the source of your smile, but sometimes your smile can be the source of your joy."

—THICH NHAT HANH

Conjure up a spark of joy by remembering the fun you used to have when playing as a child. What did you enjoy the most? How does recalling this memory help with your 90-day goal?

Life is filled with the joy of sound. What sounds bring you joy? The innocent giggle of a baby or the sound of rain on the roof? Waves at the beach or the "tip tap" of your excited dog's toenails as you come home? Describe your favorite sounds and what they mean to you.

Beauty is everywhere. You just have to remember to look for it. Look up from this journal. Does the light sparkle off a drinking glass? Is a nearby plant vibrant and full of life? Take a minute and gaze on the beauty surrounding you. Describe it.

Joy can be found in the little details. Does hot tea in an antique china cup bring you joy? Then give it to yourself. Ask for the things that bring you joy and satisfaction. Don't settle. What slice of joy will you welcome today?

You don't have to be an artist to enjoy creativity. Doodling is surprisingly enjoyable. Here's an easy task to get you started: Have fun with some random doodling in this space and see where it leads you.

What if you could wave a magic wand and gift yourself more joy? What would you wish for? What experience would be so much fun? Who would you love to share it with? How could you make it even better? Describe your dream below.

WHAT BRINGS YOU JOY?

What brings you joy? I know, I know! This is a success journal, and you want to be even more successful, but, truthfully, you're here writing and learning and growing, and that itself makes you a success.

Remember when I said success is an emotion? Well, so is joy. When you intentionally cultivate an emotion that you want, you will feel better. And when you feel better, you will take better, more courageous actions and experience more joy.

For each of the next seven nights, describe three things that brought you joy throughout the day.

Day 1:

Day 2:

Day 3:

Day 4:

Day 5:

Day 6:

Day 7:

MINDFULNESS

"Be happy in the moment, that's enough. Each moment is all we need, not more."

—MOTHER TERESA

Try mindfully drinking water. Slowly lift the glass to your mouth, sip, taste, and swallow. Describe it as if it were a completely new experience. How will this help with your 90-day goal?

Today, write down your first name, your full name, any nicknames you've gone by, and the name you like to be called. Write them very slowly and mindfully. Who calls you each version of your name? How do you feel about each one?

Sit with your back comfortably straight and put one hand on your stomach and the other on your chest. Focus on moving your abdomen while you breathe. Describe how this is different from the way you normally breathe. Did you notice a change in how you feel?

Today, spend some time outside, and instead of focusing on your thoughts, concentrate on the things you see, hear, and smell outside of yourself. What did you notice about your movement? What caught your attention? How can this exercise help you be more mindful of your surroundings?

Sit where you are right now. What five things do you see? What four things can you touch? What three things do you hear? What two things do you smell? What one thing can you taste?

List them. What did you notice that you would normally overlook?

Greet the day. Get up early to catch the sunrise. Watch the sun emerge as the sky and clouds change colors. Observe how the light slowly grows and the shadows dissolve. How did this activity make you feel? What did you enjoy most?

MINDFUL MANDALA COLORING

Coloring is soothing, and it can be a fun way to practice mindfulness. Instead of rushing to finish, enjoy the details of the process. Make coloring mindful by following these instructions.

1. Grab some colored pencils or crayons.

2. Look at the selection and choose only your favorite colors. Put the others away.

3. Color slowly, noticing the pencil on the page as it moves back and forth and leaves color behind.

4. Look carefully at the lines and the shapes that you're coloring.

5. Notice the details of the shapes and where the lines touch.

6. Pay attention to your thoughts without getting wrapped up in them. While you're coloring, watch the thoughts come into your mind and leave when they are replaced with the next thought.

GRATITUDE

"Gratitude is the healthiest of all emotions. The more you express gratitude for what you have, the more likely you will have even more to express gratitude for."

—ZIG ZIGLAR

Tag someone special on your favorite social media platform and share why you're grateful for them. How does it feel to publicly acknowledge them?

List three people you appreciate and who you have benefited from knowing. Then share why you're so lucky to know them. What are funny memories you share? What about them inspires you most? What characteristics do they have that make you smile?

Put on some music and dance! You can dance lying down, sitting, or standing—any position will do. Write how you feel about being able to do this and how grateful you are for your body.

What are the places in nature that you value the most? Name and describe your all-time favorite place. Why are you grateful for this place? What experiences have you had there, and how have they impacted who you are and who you are becoming?

What is your favorite food? Describe all the people who play a part in bringing it to your table (for example, farmers, truckers, shopkeepers, and cooks). Express your gratitude for this long and complex line of contributors.

Write a *secret* thank-you note to someone who has had a positive impact on you. Describe the difference they've made and how the world is a better place because of them. Then, mail it anonymously.

BE THANKFUL IN ALL THINGS

Gratitude reminds you to look at everything with fresh eyes. When the way you look at things in your life changes, your life changes, too. It's your perspective that creates reality, not the other way around.

Look around. What are some of the simple items you see? What everyday activities do these items allow you take part in? Use this table to capture your observations and memories.

ITEM	WHAT DO YOU NOTICE?	HOW HAVE YOU USED THIS?
Kitchen Table	*It's scratched, worn.*	*To eat meals, do my homework, and play cards and games*

How do you feel about those simple things now? Can you see how precious they are and how they enhance your life?

INNER LEADER

"I have often thought that the best way to define a man's character would be to seek out the particular mental or moral attitude in which, when it came upon him, he felt himself most deeply and intensely active and alive. At such moments there is a voice inside which speaks and says: 'This is the real me!'"

—WILLIAM JAMES

Each of us has an inner leader. It's the wise voice you hear in your mind when you get quiet. What's the name of your wise self? What does it say to you when you listen?

Do you have a memory of "hearing" that wise inner voice and following its advice? Describe the situation, what happened, and the result. What did you learn by listening to yourself and following your own sage guidance?

What challenges are getting in the way of you reaching your 90-day growth goal? Ready to take the next step toward success but you're not sure if you've got what it takes? If this sounds familiar, ask your wise self, "What would my most courageous self do?"

Get to know your inner leader. Pause and imagine you can see them in your mind's eye. How do you think they dress, sit, stand, walk? What do they look like? Are they similar to you or very different?

Your wise self is timeless and knows how to support you best. By listening and building trust in that voice, you will create an internal support system that helps you weather tough times. How do you know when you hear that voice? What are its qualities? How is it different from your usual inner monologue?

Do you have strong intuition or is it a skill you've never even considered? How would your life change if you had a wise voice that you could trust to help you day-to-day?

STORIES ARE POWERFUL—
COURAGEOUS HERO

Stories are powerful. They can also be used to quickly capture the feeling of success. When you connect with the voice of your inner mentor and the courage and grit you hold, it will help you create the next step in your success.

Remember a time from your past when you were this courageous self. Now, write the story of your victory. Cast yourself as the brave champion. Describe the obstacles you overcame, the grit and drive you needed to "keep on keeping on," and the final victory. Give the story a fun and overly dramatic title (for example, Damned Determination! or Winners Never Whine). You can even choose sweeping theme music.

QUIET YOUR INNER CRITIC

"*Most people are paralyzed by fear. Overcome it and you take charge of your life and your world.*"

—MARK VICTOR HANSEN

How often do you doubt yourself? Describe some of the areas in which you doubt your abilities. When you speak to yourself, are you harsh and critical?

Sometimes you may hear the voice of self-doubt. This is your inner critic. Use your imagination to describe your inner critic. It helps to be a little irreverent. Be gentle and have fun with this.

Draw a picture of the inner critic you described. If you don't want to draw, find a picture, cut it out, and glue it here. Give your inner critic a name, but don't be too mean. After all, it's a part of you that evolved to keep you safe.

It's completely normal to have an inner critic. Describe some of the ways that having your own personal alarm system has helped keep you safe. For example, its voice may have reminded you to prepare well for a job interview. The result was you getting to work at that fabulous company.

Treat your inner critic with a dose of compassion. Write it a comforting note, such as, *"I see you're nervous that we'll get hurt. It's okay. I'll keep you safe."* Jot down a few of these notes and repeat them to yourself when you notice negative self-talk. How will this help with your 90-day goal?

Your inner critic wants to be useful. Instead of fighting and resisting it, know that it appreciates being noticed. When you learn to calmly recognize the inner critic, you'll be able to effectively turn the volume down on the danger signal. Write three constructive phrases you will use the next time your inner critic shows up. For example, *"It's okay. I can figure this out."*

WHO ARE YOU TO BE BRILLIANT?

It's time to quiet your inner voice of self-doubt. You've chosen a 90-day growth goal. What's getting in your way of making it happen?

1. Set a timer for five minutes and write all the reasons (good, bad, justified) as to why you couldn't or shouldn't reach your 90-day growth goal.

2. Choose **one** of those thoughts and turn it around. Yes, make the thought the opposite!

3. Next, find evidence for how the "turned around thought" could already be true. Your brain acts as a search engine; when you ask it a question, it will always try to answer.

Example:

ORIGINAL THOUGHT: *I'm not ready*

TURN AROUND THOUGHT (TAT): *I am ready, right now.*

HOW IS THIS TAT TRUE? *I already have some of the skills.*
I know how to learn.
I know how to figure things out.
I'm excited about this growth goal.

CONTINUED>

Your turn:

ORIGINAL THOUGHT:

TURN AROUND THOUGHT (TAT):

HOW IS THIS TAT TRUE?

LEARN TO SAY "NO!"

"The difference between successful people and really successful people is that really successful people say no to almost everything."

—WARREN BUFFETT

Setting boundaries and learning to say "no" can be a new challenge. It's easier to start small. What is one small thing you can say "no" to today?

When you agree to everyone else's priorities, you might be saying "no" to your own. Do you find you are so easygoing that you never get to do the things you would like to do? How has that affected you? Have you considered another approach?

If you're used to being compliant and always saying "yes" to other people's requests, you may have lost track of what you like. If this sounds like you, jot down some things you used to enjoy.

Saying "no" can be uncomfortable. Do you worry that others won't like you? What might happen? Could you be excluded, or do you worry someone else will be upset? Describe a time when you declined to do something. What happened and how did you feel?

What possibilities are open for you when you prioritize your needs? Are you curious what might happen when you learn a new habit? How might saying "no" actually benefit everyone? Use this space to brainstorm possibilities.

Flip the script. Decide what you would like first. Start small, choosing how you want to spend Saturday evening. Then decide, plan, and invite other people if you want. You may find others are happy to join. Plan what you will do and how you will handle the possibility of your friends declining your invitation.

RELEASE IT

Now it's time to give yourself permission to start releasing what no longer serves you. It's only when you let something go that you open space for something new.

You don't have to release everything all at once. You can do it one small step at a time and only when you're ready. As you do, you'll feel relieved to release some of this stuff from your life.

Start by creating a small list of three or more habits and things that you're not sure you want to have around anymore. Once you've filled in the table, choose one item that you will release. Choose the easiest one, saying, *"I give myself permission to release this,"* and draw a line through it.

Examples include:

HABITS	THINGS
Social media before I get out of bed in the morning	*A pair of worn-out old shoes*
Complaining	*That pile of magazines*

YOUR LIFE PURPOSE

"For me, success is not a public thing. It's a private thing. It's when you have fewer and fewer regrets."

—TONI MORRISON

Have you ever wondered if you're here for a reason, a purpose? You're not alone. How will your life change when you discover your life's purpose? If you already feel like you have a purpose, how did that realization change things?

Yes, your life has a purpose. You might think you have to search high and low to discover it, but that's not true. Your purpose *wants* you, and it has left a trail of clues. Describe a peak experience in which everything flowed easily and felt right. What about that experience would you like to capture?

Your purpose is hiding in plain sight. What type of play did you enjoy most as a child? What made this activity so enjoyable? What did you always dream of becoming when you were growing up? What qualities do all these memories have in common?

Feeling a sense of purpose is important at all ages. Your purpose is tied to your sense of meaning. Success and purpose go hand in hand, and reaching the next level of success will *only* feel successful when it is meaningful. What meaning have you uncovered through this journal?

Dive below the surface of the purpose you're uncovering by answering these questions: What do I care about most in the world? What truly matters to me? Use this space to describe things, people, and causes that hold meaning for you.

Your purpose will evolve and shift with time. Now that you have begun to understand your purpose, reflect on what action you can take today that aligns with your purpose. How can you make an impact? How does this make you feel?

DECIDE ON PURPOSE

Part of living your purpose is making the decision that you will follow your meaningful path. You get to decide what that will be. Deciding is a superpower. When you are indecisive, you are making the decision not to move forward, and this leads to overwhelm and stagnation. Don't let that happen to you. Everything starts with a decision.

What's the biggest worry you have about making a big decision? Are you nervous you will make the wrong one? What if every decision was the right decision? Take action and you either win or you learn, which will lead you to the next decision, and the next. The path may seem a little longer because you didn't win the first time but, eventually, you will. What decision will you make today? Use the decision tree on page 161 to find out where you could go if you started taking decisive action today.

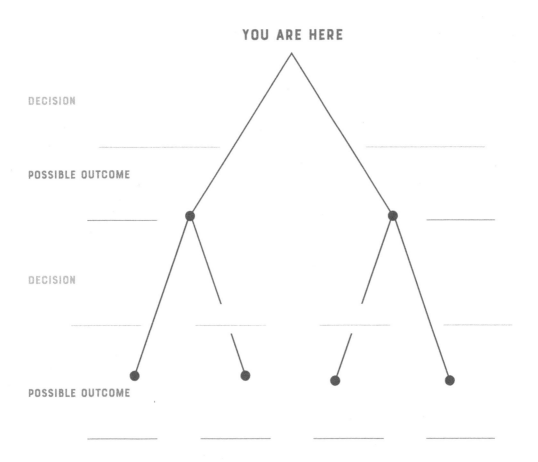

YOU ARE HERE

DECISION

_____   _____

POSSIBLE OUTCOME

_____   _____

DECISION

_____   _____

POSSIBLE OUTCOME

_____   _____

I am so pleased, I have decided to follow my purpose and this is my next step . . .

CLOSING NOTE

Earlier in this journal, you set a 90-day growth goal. What progress have you made on this goal? Look for the places you've grown. In what ways are you satisfied with your progress? Take a few minutes to reread some of what you've written in this success journal. Can you see the places you've grown and signs of the even more successful you emerging?

Don't assume other people's opinions and guidance are more valuable than your own. You have discovered your inner leader, and I would encourage you to rely on that quiet voice of wisdom to guide you.

Self-reflection and journaling are strong indicators of future success. I would highly recommend that you buy another journal and continue to build this habit of writing down your thoughts and learning from yourself. Use that writing space to create more dreams and plans and to track your progress.

You've come so far, and the next step on your journey up the mountain of life is completely up to you. Best wishes, and I am honored to have been part of your journey.

RESOURCES

This series of posts shows you how to start and keep a journal. There are writing prompts and guidelines to help you make and keep this new habit, too.
StepIntoSuccessNow.com/pages/how-to-start-a-journal

Curious about how to shift your mindset to improve your outlook on life and the outcomes, too? Listen to my podcast, *She Coaches Coaches*.
She-Coaches-Coaches.captivate.fm/listen

Vision boards are a fun and powerful way to design your life. Learn how they work and how to create your first vision board.
StepIntoSuccessNow.com/pages/vision-board

ACKNOWLEDGMENTS

Every book is the result of collaboration. My thanks go to the team at Callisto Media who collaborated in making this journal a reality. I would also like to send love and thanks to my husband, Peter, and my entire family for their continued support and encouragement in everything I do.

ABOUT THE AUTHOR

CANDY MOTZEK, CPCC, PCC, is a podcast host, author, and life and business coach. She defines success by living every day close to nature, doing work she loves and making a difference. She believes that coaching transforms lives. She helps people get unstuck and feel more confident so they can play bigger and create more meaningful success.

She is a "recovering" corporate executive and engineer who combines practical strategy and mindset in her unique calming approach.

Candy lives with her husband Peter in Vancouver, Canada, and works from her she-shed with a view of the coastal mountains. You can read more about Candy at StepIntoSuccessNow.com.

CPSIA information can be obtained
at www.ICGtesting.com
Printed in the USA
JSHW010033160322
23881JS00001B/1

9 781638 781226